Super Shred Diet Recipes

50 Delicious Recipes To SHRED Fat Fast!

Chicken, Beef, Seafood, Lamb and Vegetable Recipes.

What You Will Find In This Book

Fifty delicious "super SHRED" diet recipes that will make the whole program seem even more amazing and easier to follow.

The recipes are grouped in five categories according to their main ingredient. These include chicken, beef, lamb, seafood, and vegetables.

Super SHRED diet plan is the next generation fast weight loss program designed by Dr. Ian Smith, a world-renowned physician, researcher, and bestselling author. SUPER SHRED diet plan allows you to quickly get in shape within weeks, without compromising the integrity of your body.

The central component of the super SHRED diet plan is its flexibility. It lays a plan of action, the timings of food intake, the important foods that must be taken, and the foods that are not allowed. How you cook them is left completely to you.

The 50 different recipes that you will find in this report have been selected or designed to keep you EXACTLY ON TRACK with the super SHRED diet plan. Henceforth, you can lose weight, get in shape, and remain healthy without compromising on your sense of taste.

Table of Contents

Super SHRED Chicken Recipes **16**

Recipe #1: Chicken Parmesan with Spinach 16

Serving Size 16

Cooking Time 16

Nutritional Value 16

Ingredients 16

Directions 16

Recipe #2: Pizza de' Chicken Pesto 17

Serving Size 17

Cooking Time 17

Nutritional Value 17

Ingredients 17

Directions 17

Recipe #3: Saffron Chicken 18

Serving Size 18

Cooking Time 18

Nutritional Value 18

Ingredients 18

Directions 18

Recipe #4: Chili Chicken with Chipotles and White Beans 19

Serving Size 19

Cooking Time 19

Nutritional Value 19

Ingredients 19

Super SHRED Chicken Recipes

Recipe #1: Chicken Parmesan with Spinach

Serving Size

Serves 1

Cooking Time

6 minutes

Nutritional Value

Calories/serving: 366
Total Carbohydrate: 21 grams
Cholesterol: 70 mg
Total Fat: 17.4 grams

Ingredients

1. Chicken Breast (skinless, boneless) – 1 piece
2. Grated Parmesan – 1 tbsp
3. Baby Spinach – 3-4 leaves
4. Marinara –1/4 Cup
5. Bread Crumbs (Italian Seasoned) – 1 tbsp
6. Crushed Garlic Clove – 1
7. Olive Oil – 1 tbsp
8. Salt/Pepper – to taste

Directions

Plod the chicken until it has an even surface. Sprinkle salt and pepper, the parmesan cheese, and breadcrumbs. Use a non-stick pan to heat the oil. Add the chicken and garlic to oil. Sauté for each side for 2–3 minutes. Pour hot marinara followed by spinach. Heat till the spinach wilts. Remove from heat. Serve hot.

Recipe #2: Pizza de' Chicken Pesto

Serving Size

Serves 4

Cooking Time

10 minutes

Nutritional Value

Calories/serving: 528.2
Total Carbohydrate: 58.8 grams
Cholesterol: 47.6 mg
Total Fat: 19.6 grams

Ingredients

1. Chicken – 1 Cup (cooked and sliced)
2. Pizza Shell – One 12" prebaked shell
3. Pesto – 1/3 Cup of prepared pesto
4. Artichoke Hearts – ½ Cup (rinsed and quartered)
5. Red Pepper – 1 (roasted and grated to thin strips)
6. Goat Cheese – ½ Cup (crushed)

Directions

Preheat the oven to 450F. Sprinkle the pest over the pizza shell. Spread the artichoke hearts, chicken pieces, and pepper strips. Top it with goat cheese. Set the timer for 10 minutes or bake till you have a crisp crust. Remove from oven and serve!

Recipe #3: Saffron Chicken

Serving Size

Serves 4

Cooking Time

40 minutes

Nutritional Value

Calories/serving: 350
Total Carbohydrate: 5 grams
Cholesterol: 121 mg
Total Fat: 19 grams

Ingredients

1. Chicken Breast – 6 oz of boneless and skinless breast halves
2. Low- Fat Yogurt – 1 ½ Cups
3. Saffron – a pinch of crushed threads
4. Garlic Clove – 1 (minced)
5. Salt/Pepper – to taste

Directions

Pour the yogurt in a large bowl. Add a pinch of saffron, garlic, salt, and pepper, and mix. Add the chicken to the bowl and toss until it is completely coated.

Preheat the broiler. Leave the chicken to marinate at room temperature for 15-20 minutes. Broil the chicken until both sides are cooked brown. This means broiling each side for atleast10 minutes.

Recipe #4: Chili Chicken with Chipotles and White Beans

Serving Size

Serves 4

Cooking Time

30 minutes

Nutritional Value

Calories/serving: 431
Total Carbohydrate: 55 grams
Cholesterol: 60 mg
Total Fat: 5 grams

Ingredients

1. Chicken Breasts – 2 Cups (cooked and diced)
2. Fat Free Chicken Broth – 2 Cups
3. Chipotle Chilies – 1 Can (7 oz dipped in adobo sauce)
4. Beans – 3 Cans (rinsed and drained)
5. Chopped Onion – 1 Cup
6. Ground Cumin – 1 tsp
7. Fresh Cilantro – 1 tbsp
8. Olive Oil – 2 tsp

Directions

Mix the broth, beans, and cumin in a large pan. Heat the oil in a non-stick skittle. Add the onion and sauté to a soft pulp. Remove seeds from 1 chili, chop to fine strips. Add 2 tsp adobo sauce and the chopped chili to the broth mixture. Bring the mixture to a boil. Let it simmer for 15 minutes.

Puree one cup of the mixture in a blender/food-processor. Add puree to the pan followed by chicken. Cook for until the mixture is thoroughly heated. Stir in cilantro. Remove from heat and serve.

Recipe #5: Moroccan Chicken Stew

Serving Size

Serves 4

Cooking Time

26 minutes

Nutritional Value

Calories/serving: 355.7
Total Carbohydrate: 31.2
Cholesterol: 77.3 mg
Total Fat: 2.9 grams

Ingredients

1. Chicken Legs – 1 lb (skinless and boneless)
2. Chicken Stock – 1 Cup
3. Large Zucchini – 1 (finely cut into cubes)
4. Garbanzo Beans – 1 Can (16 ounces)
5. Diced Tomatoes – 1 Can (14.5 ounces)
6. Olive Oil – ½ tbsp
7. Salt/Pepper – to taste
8. Cayenne Pepper – ½ tsp
9. Ground Cumin – 1 tsp
10. Ground Cinnamon – ½ tsp
11. Fresh Cilantro – for dressing (chopped)

Directions

Season the chicken legs with salt and pepper. Heat the oil in a skittle and add the legs to the pan. Thoroughly cook each side to a crisp brown. Add the zucchini and continue cooking while stirring. When the zucchini has turned light brown, add the garbanzo beans, diced tomatoes, and chicken stock.

Sprinkle the powdered cumin, cinnamon, and cayenne. Turn the heat to low and let the mixture simmer for another 15 minutes. When the chicken is cooked and tender, season it to taste with more salt/pepper. Adorn with the finely chopped cilantro and serve.

Recipe #6: White Bean Chicken Stew

Serving Size

Serves 4

Cooking Time

10 minutes

Nutritional Value

Calories/serving: 273.7
Total Carbohydrate: 23.5 grams
Cholesterol: 47.1 mg
Total Fat: 8 grams

Ingredients

1. Chicken – 1 ½ Cups (cooked and diced)
2. Chopped Onion – 1 medium
3. Olive Oil – 2 tsp
4. Ground Garlic Cloves – 2
5. Ground Black Pepper – 1/8 tsp
6. Chicken Broth –2 Cups of reduced-sodium chicken broth
7. Medium Sized Zucchini – 2 (thinly sliced)
8. Cannellini Beans – 1 Can 19 oz. (rinsed and drained)
9. Prepared Pesto – 2 tbsp

Directions

Heat the oil in a non-stick pan. Cook the garlic and the onion to a pulp. Add the beans, zucchini, and pepper to the mixture. Bring the mixture to a boil. Maintain the boil for another 2 minutes. Add the chicken and let the mixture boil for another minute before removing from heat. Add the pesto and let the mixture stand for 3 more minutes to blend the flavor. Serve.

Recipe #7: Pesto Baked Chicken

Serving Size

Serves 4

Cooking Time

20 minutes

Nutritional Value

Calories/serving: 236
Total Carbohydrate: 2.5 grams
Total Fat: 11.5 grams

Ingredients

1. Basil Pesto – 4 tsp
2. Chicken Breasts – 2 Cups (Skinless and boneless)
3. Medium Tomato – 1 (diced)
4. Mozzarella Cheese (Reduced Fat) – 1.5 ounce (Grated/shredded)
5. Parmesan Cheese – 2 tsp
6. Salt/Pepper – to taste

Directions

Cut the chicken breasts into 5 thin horizontal cutlets. Add shallow cuts to each cutlet and season with salt and pepper. Place the chicken on a lined /greased baking sheet. Spread around 1 tsp of presto over the chicken.

Preheat the oven to 400 F. Place the baking sheet in oven and bake for 10 –15 minutes. Remove from oven when the chicken is longer pink. Adorn with, parmesan and mozzarella cheese, and diced tomatoes. Bake for additional 5 minutes or till the cheese melts. Serve

Recipe #8: Chicken with Mushrooms and Scallions

Serving Size

Serves 4

Cooking Time

12 minutes

Nutritional Value

Calories/serving: 190
Total Carbohydrate: 7 grams
Protein: 28 grams
Total Fat: 5 grams

Ingredients

1. Chicken Breasts – 1 lb (skinless, boneless, and cut)
2. Shiitake Mushrooms – 4 oz. (thinly diced with stems removed)
3. Water – 4 cups
4. Low-Sodium Soy Sauce – 1/4 cup
5. Scallions – 1 small bunch
6. Toasted Sesame Oil – 1 tbsp
7. Gingerroot – 1 (a 2-inch piece, peeled and diced)
8. Garlic Clove – 1 (finely chopped)

Directions

Separate the scallions into greens and whites. Heat the sesame oil over medium heat in a large pan. Add the garlic and scallion whites. Cook and stir for a minute before adding mushrooms. Cook for 3 minutes or till the mushrooms soften up. Add soy sauce, ginger, and water. Simmer the broth for 3 minutes. Add the chicken and reduce heat to low. Lid and cook for 6- 8 minutes or till the chicken is cooked through.

Remove from heat and transfer chicken to a shallow bowl. Ladle with broth and adorn with the scallion greens. Serve.

Recipe #9: Sizzling Stir-Fried Chicken

Serving Size

Serves 5

Cooking Time

10 minutes

Nutritional Value

Calories/serving: 333
Total Carbohydrate: 11 grams
Protein: 34 grams
Total Fat: 18 grams

Ingredients

1. Chicken Breasts – 1 lb (skinless, boneless, rinsed and patted dry)
2. Reduced-Sodium Chicken Broth – 3/4 cup
3. Bean Sprouts – 2 cups
4. Scallions – 1 small bunch (chopped, whites and greens separated)
5. Brown Rice – for serving (steamed)
6. Garlic Cloves – 3 (finely chopped)
7. Low-Sodium Soy Sauce – 1 1/2 tablespoons
8. Sesame Oil – 1 ½ tsp
9. Canola Oil – 1 ½ tablespoons
10. Cornstarch –1 1/2 tsp
11. Honey – 1 tsp
12. Fresh Ginger – 1 tbsp (peeled and grated)
13. Unsalted Roasted Peanuts – 1/2 cup
14. Salt – 1/2 tsp
15. Red Pepper Flakes – 1/8 tsp
16. Black Pepper – 1/2 tsp

Directions

Mix the chicken broth, cornstarch, honey, and soy sauce in a small bowl. Whisk till you have consistent broth mixture.

Slice the chicken into small 1/2-inch chunks, season with pepper and salt.

Heat the oils in a large pan over medium-high heat. In a large skillet over medium-high heat, add the canola and sesame oils. Stir-fry the chicken for 5 minutes or till it is cooked through. Remove from heat and transfer to platter.

To the same pan, add the ginger, garlic, and scallion whites. Sprinkle red pepper and cook for 30 second. Stir-fry the bean sprouts with the contents for a minute. Gradually pour the broth mixture in the saucepan. Reduce heat to simmer. Scrap stir and cook for 2 minutes, or till you have a slightly thick mixture. Add the chicken, scallion greens, and peanuts. Cook for 2 minutes. Remove from heat. Serve over brown rice.

Recipe #10: Tandoori Chicken

Serving Size

Serves

Cooking Time

2 hrs 20 minutes

Nutritional Value

Calories/serving: 152
Total Carbohydrate: 0.7 grams
Cholesterol: 74 mg
Total Fat: 2.2 grams

Ingredients

1. Skinless and Boneless Chicken Breast Halves – 4 (6 oz.)
2. Plain Reduced-Fat Yogurt – 1 ½ cups
3. Grated Onion – 2 tbsp
4. Fresh Ginger – 1 tbsp (peel and grated)
5. Canola oil – 1 tbsp
6. Ground cumin – 1 tsp
7. Ground Red Pepper – 1/2 tsp
8. Ground Turmeric – 1/4 tsp
9. Garlic Cloves – 3 (minced)
10. Salt – 1/2 tsp

Directions

Mix the yogurt with grate onions, fresh ginger, garlic cloves, canola oil, turmeric, cumin, and red pepper in a large zip top plastic bag. Dip the chicken in the bag and seal. Add to refrigerator and leave to marinate for 2 hours.

Place a small roasting pan in oven. Preheat the broiler to high. Remove chicken from the bag. Discard the marinade. Sprinkle both sides with salt and arrange the chicken in the pan. Broil for 15 minutes on lower third. Turn chicken halfway through. Remove from heat and let stand for a few minutes before serving.

Super SHRED Beef Recipes

Recipe #1: Quick Beef Gyro

Serving Size

Serves 4

Cooking Time

12 minutes

Nutritional Value

Calories/serving: 436.3
Total Carbohydrate: 44.1 grams
Cholesterol: 81.6 mg
Total Fat: 20.2 grams

Ingredients

1. Minced Lean Beef – 1 lb
2. Yogurt – 1 Cup
3. Seeded Cucumber – 1/3 (diced)
4. Small Onion – 1 (chopped)
5. Onion – 2 tbsp (finely chopped)
6. Lettuce – 3 Cups (shredded)
7. Tomato – 1 large (diced)
8. Ground Garlic Clove – 1
9. Sugar – 1 tsp
10. Dried Oregano – 1 ½ tsp
11. Garlic Powder – 1 tsp
12. Pepper – ¾ tsp
13. Pita Bread – 4

Directions

Mix the yogurt, cucumber, minced garlic clove, sugar, and 2 tsp of onion in a bowl. Refrigerate the mixture. Add the ground beef and the remaining seasoning in a separate bowl. Mix well to create a dough like content. Shape the meaty dough into 5-6 small patties.

Broil or grill the patties for 10 minutes or till the meat no longer remains pink. Slice the patties into thin slices and stuff them into pitas. Add the diced tomato, lettuce, and onion. Serve with yogurt sauce

Recipe #2: Prime Beef Rib

Serving Size

Serves 10

Cooking Time

5 hrs

Nutritional Value

Calories/serving: 17.2
Total Carbohydrate: 3.8 grams
Cholesterol: 0.0 mg
Total Fat: 0.1 grams

Ingredients

1. Prime Rib Roast – 1
2. Kosher Salt – ½ Cup
3. Rosemary – ¼ Cup
4. Garlic Powder – ¼ Cup
5. Black Pepper – 1/8 Cup (cracked)

Directions

Combine the seasoning in a bowl. Slice shallow cuts on the rib. Apply the seasoning to the rib.

Preheat the oven to 375 F. Grease a boiling pan and place the rib bone side up. Bake for 45-50 minutes, and then turn off the oven. Take out the rib and let stand idle for 15 minutes to allow the juices a thoroughly perspiration. Slowly scrap off the layer of salt. Serve with sauce.

Recipe #3: Roast Beef Chipotle

Serving Size

Serves

Cooking Time

7 hrs

Nutritional Value

Calories/serving: 346.3
Total Carbohydrate: 8.8 grams
Cholesterol: 149.6 mg
Total Fat: 21 grams

Ingredients

1. Chuck Roast – 3 pounds (trimmed)
2. Beef Broth – 1 Cup
3. Green Chilies – 1 Can (4 oz.)
4. Salsa Verde – 1 Can (7 oz.)
5. Chipotle Chilies in Adobo Sauce– 3 (chopped)
6. Onion – 1 Cup (Diced)
7. Ground Garlic – 3 tsp
8. Sal/Pepper – 1 tsp
9. Chili Powder – 2 tsp
10. Cumin – 2 tsp

Directions

Mix the broth, green chilies, sauce, and onion to a crock pot. Sprinkle the chuck with chili powder, salt, pepper, and cumin. Place the chuck in a crock pot and leave the contents to simmer on high heat for 5 hours. Remove from heat, and shred the meat with a fork. Cook for another 15 minutes. Serve with crusty rolls, or tacos.

Recipe #4: Beefy Horseradish Rolls

Serving Size

Serves 5

Cooking Time

50 minutes

Nutritional Value

Calories/serving: 41.9
Total Carbohydrate: 2.6 grams
Cholesterol: 9.9 mg
Total Fat: 4 grams

Ingredients

1. Deli Beef – 8 oz. (sliced)
2. Cream Cheese – 1 Pack (8 oz.)
3. Fresh Parsley – ¼ Cup
4. Green Onions – 2 around ½ a Cup (Chopped)
5. Horseradish – 2 tbsp (rinsed and drained)
6. Flour Tortillas – 2 (10")
7. Garlic Powder – ¼ tsp
8. Salt –1/4 tsp

Directions

In a bowl, mix parsley, onions, and horseradishes to the cream cheese. Spread the paste on the two tortillas. Add the deli beef slices. Wrap and roll in a plastic wrap. Refrigerate for a day or till firm. Cut the roll into half-inch slices and serve.

Recipe #5: Roasted Beef

Serving Size

Serves 4

Cooking Time

8 hours

Nutritional Value

Calories/serving: 295.2
Total Carbohydrate: 2.6 grams
Cholesterol: 149.8 mg
Total Fat: 13.6 grams

Ingredients

1. Beef Roast – 2 pounds
2. Dry Gravy Mix (brown) – 1 pack (5/8 oz.)
3. Ranch Dressing – 1 pack (5/8 oz.)
4. Water –¼ Cups

Directions

Mix the dried gravy and ranch dressing in a bowl. Place the roast beef in a crock-pot. Sprinkle the gravy-ranch mix on the roast beef. Pour water and place the crock-pot on low heat. Cook for 7-8 hours. Remove from crock-pot, and serve with sauce.

Recipe #6: Quick and Crisp Beef Chimichangas

Serving Size

Serves 3

Cooking Time

20 minutes

Nutritional Value

Calories/serving: 373.6
Total Carbohydrate: 24.7 grams
Cholesterol: 71.7 mg
Total Fat: 32 grams

Ingredients

1. Minced Beef – 1 pound
2. 8-iinch Flour Tortilla – 8
3. Butter – ¼ Cup
4. Onion – 1 med (chopped)
5. Pace Salsa/Picante Sauce – ¾ Cup
6. Dried and Crushed Oregano Leaves – ½ tsp
7. Salt – ½ tsp
8. Garlic Clove – 2 (ground)
9. Ground Cumin – 2 tsp

Directions

Preheat the oven to 475 F. Mix the beef, onion, garlic and meet. Brown the mix in the oven then drain. Mix the salt, cumin, and oregano to the salsa sauce. Add the drained beef mixture. Stir and then simmer for 5 minutes to remove the liquid.

Butter one side of the tortilla and spread the beef mixture to the unbuttered side. Fold both ends and completely cover the filling. Place the filled tortilla in a baking dish, seem-side down. Bake until the tortillas become a golden brown (15 minutes). Remove from heat and serve with salsa sauce (avoid guacamole sauce)

Recipe #7: Juicy Salisbury Steak

Serving Size

Serves 6

Cooking Time

30 minutes

Nutritional Value

Calories/serving: 331.9
Total Carbohydrate: 13.8 grams
Cholesterol: 108.1 mg
Total Fat: 26 grams

Ingredients

1. Condensed French Onion Soup – 1 Can (10 ½ oz.)
2. Ground Beef – 1 ½ Pounds
3. Dried Breadcrumbs – ½ Cup
4. Ketchup – ¼ Cup
5. Water – ¼ Cup
6. Egg – 1
7. Salt – ¼ tsp
8. Ground Black Pepper – to taste
9. Mustard Powder – ½ tsp
10. Flour – 1 tbsp
11. Worcestershire Sauce – 2-3 tsp or to taste

Directions

Beat the egg with salt and pepper. Mix the beaten egg, ground beef and bread crumbs to one-third cup soup in a bowl till you have a dough. Shape the dough in to small patties.

In a bowl, mix the remaining soup with flour to gain a smooth consistent blend. Add water, ketchup, mustard powder, and Worcestershire sauce. Mix to gain a consistent mixture.

Brown both sides of all the patties in a non-stick saucepan. Remove all excess fat from the saucepan. Pour the soup/sauce mixture in the sauce pan. Lid the pan and cook for another 20 minutes while occasionally stirring. Serve hot.

Recipe #8: Mexico's Beef Stuffed Shells

Serving Size

Serves

Cooking Time

35 minutes

Nutritional Value

Calories/serving: 141.4
Total Carbohydrate: 7.4 grams
Cholesterol: 31.7 mg
Total Fat: 11.7 grams

Ingredients

1. Large Pasta Shells – 12 -14 (cooked)
2. Minced Beef – 1 pound
3. Water – ½ Cup
4. Salsa – 1 ½ Cup (divided)
5. Cheddar/Jalapeno Cheese – 1 Cup (shredded)
6. Tomato Sauce – ¾ Quart (750 ml)
7. Chili Powder – to taste
8. Medium Onion – 1 (diced)
9. Green Onion – for garnish

Directions

Brown the beef and drain, do not rinse. Sprinkle all the seasoning, onion, ¼ a cup of cheese, pour water and mix. Mix salsa and tomato sauce with chili powder. Add to the ground beef. Prepare the baking pan (9x12) by spreading a thin layer of sauce.

Fill each pasta shell with the minced beef and mixture and place in a separate dish. Top with the remaining sauce. Garnish with green onion and sprinkle with cheese. Wrap with plastic and freeze. Defrost and bake for 30 minutes at 350 F. Sprinkle additional cheese before serving.

Recipe #9: Beefed Sloppy Joe

Serving Size

Serves 6

Cooking Time

1 hour 20 minutes

Nutritional Value

Calories/serving: 346.5
Total Carbohydrate: 14.2 grams
Cholesterol: 80.4 grams
Total Fat: 31.6 grams

Ingredients

1. Ground Round/Beef– 1 ½ pounds
2. Catsup – ¾ Cup
3. Small Onion – 1 (finely chopped)
4. Mustard – 2 tbsp
5. Vinegar – 2 tbsp
6. Worcestershire Sauce – 2 tbsp
7. Sugar – 2 tbsp
8. Salt – to taste

Directions

Add the onion and salt to the ground beef. Cook on low heat for 15 minutes. Mix the remaining ingredients to the skillet and cook for another 10 minutes. Drain and let the mixture simmer for one hour with occasional stirs. Spread on buns and serve.

Recipe #10: Filet Mignon Glazed With Balsamic

Serving Size

Serves 4

Cooking Time

20 minutes

Nutritional Value

Calories/serving: 215
Total Carbohydrate: 4.7 grams
Cholesterol: 70 mg
Total Fat: 9.2 grams

Ingredients

1. Beef Tenderloin Steaks – 4 (4 oz.)
2. Dry Sherry – 3 tbsp
3. Bottled Minced Garlic – 2 tsp
4. Low-Sodium Soy Sauce – 2 tbsp
5. Pomegranate Balsamic Vinegar – 1 tbsp
6. Honey – 2 tsp
7. Salt – 1/4 tsp
8. Freshly Ground Black Pepper – 1/4 tsp
9. Crushed Red Pepper – 1/8 tsp

Directions

Season the steaks on both sides with salt and black pepper. Coat a large non-stick saucepan with cooking spray and heat over medium-high heat. Cook each side of the steak for 3 minutes or until it is to your liking. Remove from skillet and cover.

Sauté red pepper and garlic for 30 seconds. Add sherry and bring to a boil. Cook for another 30 seconds before adding soy sauce. Add the vinegar and honey. Stir occasionally till it is brought to a boil. Reduce heat and cook for another minute. Serve with warm steaks.

Super SHRED Seafood Recipes

Recipe #1: Salmon Glazed With Bourbon

Serving Size

Serves

Cooking Time

20 minutes

Nutritional Value

Calories/serving: 353
Total Carbohydrate: 13 grams
Cholesterol: 87 mg
Total Fat: 14.1 grams

Ingredients

1. Skinless Salmon Fillet – 4 (6 oz.)
2. Green Onions – 1/4 cup (thinly sliced)
3. Brown Sugar –3 tbsp
4. Bourbon – 3 tbsp
5. Low-Sodium Soy Sauce – 2 tbsp
6. Fresh Ginger – 1 tbsp (peeled and grated)
7. Fresh Lime Juice – 1 tbsp
8. Garlic Cloves – 3 (minced)
9. Freshly Ground Black Pepper – 1/4 tsp
10. Sesame Seeds – 1tbsp (toasted)

Directions

In a zip-top plastic bag or an airtight container, mix the soya sauce with bourbon, sugar, ginger, lime, and garlic cloves. Add the fillets, roll to completely coat, then refrigerate for 1 ½ hours to marinate.

Spray a large non-stick saucepan with cooking spray. Heat it over medium-high heat. Place fish and marinade to pan. Cook each side for at least four minutes or until the fish flakes easily when tested with a fork. Drizzle each fillet with about 2 tsp of sauce. Sprinkle ¾ tbsp of sesame seeds and 1 tbsp green onions. Serve.

Recipe #2: Fish Flaked Tacos

Serving Size

Serves 4

Cooking Time

7 minutes

Nutritional Value

Calories/serving: 235
Total Carbohydrate: 28 grams
Cholesterol: 62 mg
Total Fat: 6 grams

Ingredients

1. Firm White Fish Fillet (Mahi-Mahi or other) – 3/4 lbs
2. Fajita Seasoning – 2 tsp
3. Green Cabbage – 2 cups (6 oz. thinly sliced)
4. Fresh Lime Juice – 1 tbsp
5. Salt – 1/2 tsp
6. Freshly Chopped Cilantro – 3 tbsp
7. Corn Tortillas – 8 (6-inch)
8. Reduced-Fat Sour Cream – 2 ½ tbsp
9. Avocado – ½ (pitted and diced)
10. Bottled salsa – for serving
11. Lime wedges – from 2-3 limes

Directions

Use the fajita seasoning to sprinkle coat both sides of the fillets. Preheat the grill after spraying it with cooking spray.

In a small bowl, add the cilantro, salt, lime juice, and cabbage. Mix thoroughly. Microwave the tortillas. First, wrap in paper towels and microwave until they are warm.

Grill the fillets for at least for 4 minutes on each side or till you can easily flake the fish with a fork. Flake the fish just before topping the tortillas.

Spread the warm tortillas. Coat with 1 tsp of sour cream followed by the cilantro-cabbage mixture. Top with flaked fish fillets. Serve with lime wedges and salsa.

Recipe #3: Crab Salad Melts

Serving Size

Serves 4

Cooking Time

25 minutes

Nutritional Value

Calories/serving: 251
Total Carbohydrate: 30 grams
Cholesterol: 52 mg
Total Fat: 6 grams

Ingredients

1. Snow Peas OR Asparagus Spears– 1/3 cup (trimmed and thinly sliced)
2. Crabmeat – 8 oz. (with cartilage/shell removed)
3. Celery – 1/3 cup (finely chopped)
4. Swiss cheese – 1/2 cup (shredded)
5. Red Bell Pepper – 1/4 cup (finely chopped)
6. Lemon Juice – 4 tsp
7. Whole-Wheat English Muffins – 4 (split and toasted)
8. Scallion – 1 (finely chopped)
9. Low-Fat Mayonnaise – 1 tbsp
10. Old Bay seasoning – 1/4 tsp
11. Hot Sauce – 4-5 dashes
12. Freshly ground pepper – to taste

Directions

Pour 1 tsp of water to a medium microwave bowl. Add the snow peas/asparagus. Lid and microwave for 30 seconds or until they become tender. Add the celery, hot sauce, old bay seasoning, lemon juice, bell pepper, crab, scallion, mayonnaise, and pepper. Stir.

Prepare a large baking sheet and arrange the English muffin halves with their cut side up. On each half, spread about 1/4th cup of the crab salad. Sprinkle 1 tbsp of grated cheese. Pre heat the broiler. Add the rack in the oven's upper third row. Broil for 4- 6 minutes until the cheese melts.

Recipe #4: Garlic-Lemon Vegetables and Shrimps

Serving Size

Serves 4

Cooking Time

35 minutes

Nutritional Value

Calories/serving: 226
Total Carbohydrate: 14 grams
Cholesterol: 174 mg
Total Fat: 7 grams

Ingredients

1. Raw Shrimp – 1 lbs (25-30, peeled and deveined)
2. Large Red Bell Peppers – 2 (diced)
3. Asparagus – 2 lbs (trimmed and sliced 1-inch length)
4. Reduced-Sodium Chicken Broth – 1 cup
5. Extra-Virgin Olive Oil – 4 tsp (divided)
6. Lemon Juice – 2 tbsp
7. Chopped Fresh Parsley – 2 tbsp
8. Cornstarch – 1 tsp
9. Salt – 1/2 tsp (divided)
10. Freshly Grated Lemon Zest – 2 tsp
11. Cloves Garlic – 5 (minced)

Directions

Heat the garlic in the remaining oil. Cook for half a minute or more until it becomes fragrant. Add the shrimp. Stir while cooking for a minute. Add the cornstarch to the broth and whisk until you have a smooth and consistent mixture. Pour the mixture to the pan. Add ¼ tsp of salt. Cook until the shrimps are slightly cooked through (pinkish) and you have a thick sauce. Cook for another 2-minutes before removing from heat. Add the lemon juice and parsley. Stir.

Over medium-high heat in a large non-stick saucepan, heat 2 tbsp of oil. Add the asparagus, lemon zest, bell peppers, and 1/4 tsp salt. Cook for about 6 minutes or until they turn tender and cook. Occasionally stir to prevent over cooking. Remove from heat and store in a large bowl. Cover to keep warm. Serve the saucy shrimps with vegetables.

Recipe #5: Seared Tuna Drowned In Soba Noodle Salad

Serving Size

Serves 6

Cooking Time

15 minutes

Nutritional Value

Calories/serving: 256
Total Carbohydrate: 28.2 grams
Cholesterol: 34 mg
Total Fat: 6.3 grams

Ingredients

1. Uncooked Soba/Buckwheat Noodles – 6 oz.
2. Tuna Steak – 1 (1 lbs sushi-grade)
3. Shredded Carrot – 1 cup
4. English cucumber – 1 cup (finely chopped)
5. Radishes – 1/2 cup (julienne diced)
6. Red Bell Pepper – 1/3 cup (finely chopped)
7. Green Onions – 1/4 cup (finely chopped)
8. Rice Vinegar – 3 tbsp
9. Low-Sodium Soy Sauce – 2 tbsp
10. Sesame Seeds – 2 tbsp (toasted)
11. Sugar – 1 tsp
12. Freshly Ground Black Pepper – 1/4 tsp
13. Crushed Red Pepper – 1/2 tsp
14. Salt – 1/2 teaspoon (divided)
15. Dark Sesame Oil – 1 1/2 tsp
16. Peanut Oil – 1 tbsp

Directions

Boil the soba noodles. Under cold water, drain, rinse, and set aside. Coat a large skillet with cooking spray. Place it over medium-high heat. Season the tuna on both sides using ¼ tsp of pepper and salt. Cook the tuna for at least 3 minutes on each side, or more to a desired crispness and tenderness. When done, remove from heat and cut into five equal pieces. Transfer to a platter.

Add the cucumber, and remaining ingredients (except the sesame seeds) in a large bowl. Sprinkle the remaining slat and toss vigorously to mix. To serve, spread 1 cup of noodle mixture to each plate. Add a piece of tuna. Top sesame seeds.

Recipe #6: Red Snapper Creole

Serving Size

Serves 4

Cooking Time

30 min

Nutritional Value

Calories/serving: 228
Total Carbohydrate: 6.5 grams
Cholesterol: 63 mg
Total Fat: 5.8 grams

Ingredients

1. Red Snapper Fillets – 4 (6 oz.)
2. Olive Oil – 1 tbsp
3. Onion – 1/4 cup (chopped)
4. Green Bell Pepper – 1/4 cup (chopped)
5. Whole Tomatoes –1 can (14 ½ oz. un-drained and chopped)
6. Red Wine Vinegar –2 tsp
7. Low-Sodium Worcestershire Sauce – 2 tsp
8. Garlic Clove – 1 (minced)
9. Dried Basil – 1/2 tsp
10. Freshly Ground Black Pepper – 1/4 tsp
11. Salt – 1/4 tsp
12. Hot Sauce – 1-2 dash
13. Basil sprigs – for serving

Directions

Over medium-high heat, heat the oil in a large nonstick saucepan. Sauté the green bell pepper, garlic, and onions, until they are tender. Add the tomatoes, vinegar, basil,

Worcestershire sauce, salt, and hot sauce. Heat till it is brought to a boil. Add the fillets and continuously spoon the mixture over it.

Reduce heat; cover and let simmer for 10 minutes or till you can easily lake the fish with fork. Remove from heat and transfer to a serving platter. Serve immediately with basil frigs as garnish.

Recipe #7: Mussels and Linguine

Serving Size

Serves 2

Cooking Time

30 minutes

Nutritional Value

Calories/serving: 376
Total Carbohydrate: 62.2 grams
Cholesterol: 16 mg
Total Fat: 7.3 grams

Ingredients

1. Extra Virgin Olive Oil – 2 teaspoons
2. Fennel Bulb - 1/2 cup (chopped to small cubes)
3. Onion – 1/2 cup (finely chopped)
4. Fresh garlic cloves – 2 (minced)
5. Tomato – 1 cup (diced)
6. Dry vermouth – 1 cup
7. Fresh Parsley – 3 tbsp (chopped)
8. Tomato paste – 1 tbsp
9. Fresh Thyme Leaves – 1 tsp
10. Salt – 1/4 teaspoon
11. Ground Red Pepper – 1/8 tsp
12. Fresh Mussels – 28 (scrubbed and de-bearded)
13. Water – 2 tbsp
14. Cornstarch – 2 tsp
15. Uncooked Linguine – 2 cups

Directions

Spray a large non-stick saucepan with cooking spray. Heat the olive oil over medium heat. Add the chopped onions, garlic, and fennel bulbs. Sauté the mixture for 5 minutes. Add the dry vermouth, parsley, tomato paste, diced tomatoes, thyme leaves, salt, and red pepper. Bring the mixture to a boil before adding the mussels.

Lid the pan and cook till the shells bloom open, max 4 minutes. Remove the pan from heat. Remove all the shells that remain unopened. Let the mussels cool. Separate 10 shells with their meat intact. Remove meat from the remaining and add to the tomato mixture. Discard shells.

Mix the cornstarch and water. Slowly whisk until you have a consistent mixture. Add the sauce to the tomato mixture. Bring the mixture to a boil. Further cook the mixture for 2 minutes, stir continuously. Remove from heat and prepare to serve. Spread 1 cup past to each serving plate. Top with a mussel shells and cup of sauce. Serve hot.

Recipe #8: Scallops Brothed in Tarragon and Saffron

Serving Size

Serves 4

Cooking Time

35 minutes

Nutritional Value

Calories/serving: 202
Total Carbohydrate: 18 grams
Cholesterol: 39 mg
Total Fat: 4 grams

Ingredients

1. Large Dry Sea Scallops – 1 lbs (patted and dried)
2. Saffron threads –1/4 teaspoon
3. Chopped Fresh Tarragon –2 tsp
4. Extra-Virgin Olive Oil – 2 tsp
5. Onion – 1/2 cup (thinly sliced)
6. Celery– 2 stalks – (thinly sliced)
7. Garlic Cloves – 2 (thinly sliced)
8. Pomegranate Juice – 1/4 cup
9. Baby Red Potatoes – 8 oz. (sliced into 1/4-inch-thick rounds)
10. Reduced-Sodium Chicken Broth – 1 cup
11. Grape Tomatoes – 1 cup (halved)
12. Tomato Juice – (scant 3/4 cup)
13. Salt – 1/4 teaspoon

Directions

In a large non-stick saucepan, heat the oil over medium-high heat. Sprinkle the scallops with salt. Add to pan and cook each side for 2 minutes, or till they are light brown. Remove from heat and transfer to a plate.

Add the celery, garlic, and onion, to the pan. Cook for about 2 minutes until they begin to soften. Pour the pomegranate juice. Simmer for 1 minute. Add broth, tomatoes, tomato juice, saffron, and potatoes. Stir and bring to a boil. Reduce heat to a simmer, lid and cook for 10 -13 minutes, or till the potatoes become soft.

Add tarragon and scallops. Lid the pan and cook for 3 minutes or till the scallops are cooked through. Remove from heat. Serve warm.

Recipe #9: Aqua Yakitori with Scallops

Serving Size

Serves 2

Cooking Time

1 hr 45 min

Nutritional Value

Calories/serving: 229
Total Carbohydrate: 19 grams
Cholesterol: 47 mg
Total Fat: 1 gram

Ingredients

1. Dry Scallops – 6 - 12 (approx 10 oz. with muscle removed and sliced in halves)
2. Medium Button Mushrooms – 8 (halved)
3. Scallions – 6 (trim the whites and separate the greens)
4. Reduced-Sodium Soy Sauce – 2 tbsp
5. Mirin – 2 tbsp
6. Pomegranate Juice – 2 tbsp
7. Sugar – 1 tsp
8. Fresh Ginger – 1/2 tsp (minced)
9. Worcestershire sauce – 1/2 tsp
10. Molasses – 1/2 tsp

Directions

In a small skittle, add the molasses, sugar, Worcestershire and soy sauce, mirin, and ginger. Bring to a simmer and then cook for 3 minutes or till the mixture is reduced to approximately 1/4th of a cup. Remove from heat and pour in a medium bowl. Reserve 2 tbsp of sauce for basting.

Place the mushrooms and the scallops in the sauce to coat. Marinate for 25-30 minutes by covering and refrigerating the bowl. Marinating any longer will cause the scallops to tear. Prepare the yakitori by alternating mushroom halves and scallops. Prepare the scallops by first wrapping a scallion around them. While threading on the skewers, thread the from the sides to prevent rolling. Alternate 3 scallops and 4 mushroom halves.

Oil the grill rack with a folded paper towel. Preheat the grill over medium heat. Grill the scallops for 3 minutes each or till they are firm enough. Use the reserved sauce to baste the skewers while turning. Serve the sea yakitori while hot.

Recipe #10: Prawns

Serving Size

Serves 4

Cooking Time

2 hrs 30 min

Nutritional Value

Calories/serving: 314
Total Carbohydrate: 18 grams
Cholesterol: 259 mg
Total Fat: 10 grams

Ingredients

1. Large Sweet Onions – 2 (sliced)
2. Extra-Virgin Olive Oil – 2 tbsp
3. Kosher Salt – 1 tsp
4. Fresh Orange Zest – 1 tsp (grated)
5. Orange – 1 (juiced)
6. Balsamic Vinegar – 2 tbsp
7. Fresh Rosemary – 1 tsp (finely chopped)
8. Crushed Red Pepper – a pinch
9. Raw Shrimps – 12 (2-3 lbs, peeled and deveined)
10. Scallion Greens – 1/4 cup (sliced)

Directions

Preheat oven to 400F. In a 9 x 13 inch baking pan, add the onions and sprinkle with salt and oil. Toss to coat. Cover with foil and bake for 40 minutes. Check to see if they are tender. Bake uncovered for an additional 20-30 minutes or until the edges turn golden. Sprinkle crushed pepper; add the orange juice, rosemary, vinegar, and orange zest. Stir, and bake for 25 minutes to evaporate liquid. Add the shrimp, and bake for 20-25 minutes until cooked through. Add the scallion greens, stir, and serve.

Super SHRED Lamb Recipes

Recipe #1: Roasted Vegetables with Herbed Lamb Cutlets

Serving Size

Serves 4

Cooking Time

45 minutes

Nutritional Value

Calories/serving: 429
Total Carbohydrate: 23 grams
Protein: 19 grams
Total Fat: 29 grams

Ingredients

1. Lean Lamb Cutlets – 8
2. Large sweet potato – 1 (peeled and diced into chunks)
3. Courgette – 2 (diced into chunky pieces)
4. Fresh Red/Green Peppers – 2 (deseeded and diced into chunks)
5. Red Onion – 1 (diced into wedges)
6. Chopped Mint Leaves – 2 tbsp
7. Extra Virgin Olive Oil – 1 tbsp
8. Chopped Thyme Leaves– 1 tbsp

Directions

Trim the lamb cutlets of as much fat as possible. Mix herbs and freshly ground black pepper. Pat the lamb cutlets with the mixture.

Heat the oven to 400 F. In a large baking tray, arrange the courgettes, sweet potato, onion, and peppers. Drizzle with oil and season with black pepper. Roast for 25 minutes. Remove from oven and slide the vegetables to one side of the tray.

Arrange the cutlets on the remaining portion of the tray. Roast in oven for 20 minutes, turning the cutlets over after 10 minutes. Roast until the cutlets and the vegetables are tender and lightly charred.

Recipe #2: Seared Lamb Glazed with Balsamic Sauce

Serving Size

Serves 4

Cooking Time

32 minutes

Nutritional Value

Calories/serving: 253
Total Carbohydrate: 5.9 grams
Cholesterol: 90 mg
Total Fat: 11.6 grams

Ingredients

1. Lamb Loin Chops – 8 (4 oz. trimmed of all fat)
2. Finely Chopped Red Onion – 1 cup
3. Fat-Free Lower-Sodium Beef Broth –1/3 cup
4. Pomegranate Molases – 1/4 cup
5. Olive Oil – 2 tsp
6. Balsamic Vinegar – 2 tbsp
7. Chopped Garlic Cloves – 2
8. Kosher Salt – 1/2 tsp
9. Freshly Ground Black Pepper – 1/4 tsp

Directions

Season lamb loin chops with pepper and salt. Heat the oil over medium-high heat in a large non-stick saucepan. Cook the chops for 3 minutes each side or until they are browned or to your liking. Add the garlic and chopped onions to pan. Cook for another 3 minutes or until the onions are soft.

Turn lamb over, and cook 4 minutes or until desired degree of doneness. Remove lamb from pan; keep warm. Add chopped onion and garlic to pan; cook 3 minutes or until onion is tender. Add the molasses wine and bring to boil. Cook for 3 minutes or till the liquid evaporates. Stir in vinegar, bring to boil and cook till the sauce is reduced to two-thirds of a cup. Serve with lamb.

Recipe #3: Moroccan Pita Sandwiches

Serving Size

Serves 4

Cooking Time

25 minutes

Nutritional Value

Calories/serving: 370
Total Carbohydrate: 39.6 grams
Cholesterol: 31 mg
Total Fat: 9.1 grams

Ingredients

1. Ground Round – 12 oz.
2. Finely Chopped Onion – 1/3 cup
3. Tomato Slices – 16 (Cut to 1/4-inch-thickness)
4. Fat-Free Greek-Style Yogurt – 1 cup
5. 6-inch Pitas – 4 (halved)
6. Green Lettuce Leaves – 4
7. Large Egg – 1
8. Tomato Paste –2 tbsp
9. Sesame Seed Paste (Tahini) –2 tsp
10. Garlic Clove – 1 (minced)
11. Fresh Lemon Juice – 1 tsp
12. Salt – 1/2 tsp
13. Grated Lemon Rind – 1/2 tsp
14. Crushed Fennel Seeds – 1/2 tsp
15. Ground Coriander – 1/2 tsp
16. Ground Cumin – 1/4 tsp
17. Ground Cinnamon – 1/4 tsp
18. Ground Ginger – 1/8 tsp

19. Salt – 1/8 tsp

Directions

Preheat the oven to 400 F. Prepare patties by combining the ground round with the onions, tomato paste, ground coriander, cumin, cinnamon, and ginger. Beat the egg with salt and add to the round dough. Divide the dough into 8-10 equal portion and pat into 1/4th inch thick patties.

Heat a large non-stick saucepan over medium heat and coat with cooking spray. Add 3-4 patties to the skillet and cook, turning occasionally until browned (5 minutes or more). Arrange all the patties on a baking sheet. Bake for 5 minutes or until done.

Make sauce by adding tahini, lemon rind and juice, garlic clove, and salt to the yogurt. Serve each patty by topping it with 2 tbsp of sauce, 2 tomato slices, and a lettuce leaf.

Recipe #4: Blue Cheese Salad with Barbecued Sirloin

Serving Size

Serves 4

Cooking Time

30 minutes

Nutritional Value

Calories/serving: 269
Total Carbohydrate: 9.4 grams
Cholesterol: 57 mg
Total Fat: 12.4 grams

Ingredients

1. Lean Sirloin Steak – 1lb (trimmed)
2. Torn Bibb lettuce – 6 cups
3. Red Bell Pepper Strips –1 cup
4. Thinly Sliced Shallots – 1/2 cup
5. Crumbled Blue Cheese – 2 oz. (1/2 cup)
6. Thinly Sliced Peeled Cucumber – 3/4 cup
7. Chili Powder – 2 tsp
8. Sherry Vinegar – 2 tbsp
9. Dijon Mustard – 2 tsp
10. Extra-Virgin Olive Oil –1 tbsp
11. Garlic Powder – 1/2 tsp
12. Salt – ½ tsp (divided)
13. Ground Cumin – 3/4 tsp
14. Black Pepper – ¼ tsp (divided)

Directions

Coat a grill pan with cooking spray and put over medium-high heat. Combine ¼ tsp salt, garlic powder, cumin, chili powder, and 1/8 tsp black pepper. Rub evenly on both sides of the steak. Add the steak and cook for 5 minutes. Turn the side and further cook for 5 minutes. Remove from heat and let stand for 5 minutes. On a cutting board cut across grain into thin slices.

In a small bowl, whisk together the vinegar with the remaining salt and pepper. Add the oil in a drizzle while stirring. In a large bowl, combine bell pepper, shallots, cucumber, and lettuce. Drizzle with the vinaigrette and toss. Add steak and cheese as topping to salad. Serve.

Recipe #5: Spicy Pomegranate Tzatziki and Lamb Skewers

Serving Size

Serves 16

Cooking Time

8 minutes

Nutritional Value

Calories/serving: 50
Total Carbohydrate: 2 grams
Protein: 5 grams
Total Fat: 3 grams

Ingredients

1. Lamb – 300 grams (diced)
2. Greek Yogurt – ½ tsp
3. Shallot – 1 (Chopped)
4. Small Handful Mint – (chopped)
5. Pomegranates Seeds – 50 grams
6. Finger-Length Piece Cucumber – 1 (diced)
7. Garlic Clove – 1 (chopped)
8. Ground Cinnamon, Coriander, Cumin, and Garam Masala – ½ tsp
9. Honey – 1 tsp (to taste)

Directions

Prepare the tzatziki by mixing garlic, mint, cucumber, honey, and shallot with yogurt. Sprinkle pomegranate seeds. Mix the lamb with garam masala, coriander, cumin, and cinnamon.

Prepare the grill on medium-high heat. Cook the lamb for 8 minutes (4 minutes on each side). Before serving, thread the lamb onto a cocktail stick. Serve with tzatziki.

Recipe #6: Herby Couscous with Citrus & Pomegranate Dressing

Serving Size

Serves 4

Cooking Time

15 minutes

Nutritional Value

Calories/serving: 189
Total Carbohydrate: 32 grams
Protein: 4 grams
Total Fat: 6 grams

Ingredients

1. Couscous – 200 grams
2. Water – 200 ml
3. Pomegranates Seeds – 5 oz
4. Chopped Mint and Coriander – a handful
5. Orange Juice – of one large orange
6. Balsamic Vinegar – 2 tbsp
7. Olive Oil – 2 tbsp

Directions

Bring water to a boil. Place the couscous in a shallow bowl. Pour the boiling water, firmly cover and leave for 5 minutes or until the couscous absorbs all water and swells.

Prepare the dressing by combining olive oil with vinegar, and orange juice. Separate grain of the couscous with fork. First, add the herbs and pomegranate seeds. Then stir in the dressing. Season well with salt and serve.

Recipe #7: A Fruity Lamb Tagine

Serving Size

Serves 4

Cooking Time

1 hr 30 min

Nutritional Value

Calories/serving: 497
Total Carbohydrate: 46 grams
Protein: 40 grams
Total Fat: 18 grams

Ingredients

1. Chicken Stock – 600 ml
2. Lean Lamb – 500g (diced)
3. Canned Chickpeas – 400 grams(rinsed and drained)
4. Canned Chopped Tomatoes – 400 grams
5. Dried Apricots – 200 grams
6. Large Carrots –2 (lengthwise quartered and diced into chunks)
7. Large Onion – 1 (roughly chopped)
8. Garlic Cloves – 2 (finely chopped)
9. Ras-El-Hanout Spice Mix – 2 tbsp
10. Olive Oil – 2 tbsp

Directions

Preheat the oven to 350 F. Heat the oil in a casserole and cook each side of the lamb until brown. Scoop the lamb out to a separate plate. Cook the carrots and onion in the oil for 3 minutes or until golden brown. Sprinkle garlic and cook for another minute. Add tomatoes and spices. Stir and season.

Add the apricots, chickpeas, and lamb. Pour the stock and bring to a simmer while stirring. Lid the dish and bake in oven for 1 hour or until it is tender. Sprinkle and garnish with pomegranate and herbs. Serve with rice and couscous.

Recipe #8: Enchilada Casserole

Serving Size

Serves 4

Cooking Time

30 minutes

Nutritional Value

Calories/serving: 377
Total Carbohydrate: 32.4 grams
Cholesterol: 76 mg
Total Fat: 14.6 grams

Ingredients

1. Ground Sirloin – 1 lb
2. Chopped Onion – 1 cup
3. Butter – 1 tbsp
4. Minced Garlic – 1 tbsp
5. All-Purpose Flour – 1 1/2 tbsp
6. Fat-Free, Lower-Sodium Beef Broth –1 cup
7. Reduced-Sodium Taco Seasoning Mix– 1 tbsp
8. Salt-Free Tomato Sauce – 1 can (8 oz.)
9. 8-inch Whole-Wheat Flour Tortillas – 4
10. Shredded Monterey Jack Cheese With Jalapeño Peppers – 1/3 cup (1 ½ oz.)

Directions

Heat a large non-stick saucepan over medium-high heat. Add onion and beef. Cook while stirring for 6 minutes. In a medium skillet, melt butter over medium-high heat. Sauté with garlic for a minute. Add flour cook while stirring for 30 seconds. Pour tomato sauce, broth, and taco seasoning. Bring the mixture to a boil followed by 2 minutes of cooking. Reserve ½ cup of the mixture. To the beef mixture, pour 1 ½ cups of tomato mixture.

Preheat oven to 400 F. In a 9-inch pie plate, place 1 tortilla. Pour and spread 1 cup beef mixture over the tortilla. Repeat in layers with a tortilla on top. Pour and spread the remaining tomato mixture over the tortilla and top with cheese. Bake for 12 min or until cheese melts. Slice into 4 long wedges. Serve warm.

Recipe #9: Chopped With Pomegranate-Pistachio Couscous

Serving Size

Serves 4

Cooking Time

40 minutes

Nutritional Value

Calories/serving: 485
Total Carbohydrate: 44 grams
Total Fat: 18 grams

Ingredients

1. Cilantro leaves – 1 cup
2. Garlic cloves –2
3. Ground cumin – 1 tbsp
4. Cayenne pepper – 1/4 tsp
5. Fresh lemon juice – 1/4 cup
6. Pomegranate Seeds – 1/4 cup
7. Pomegranate Juice – 1/4 cup
8. finely grated lemon zest – 1 tsp
9. Extra-Virgin Olive Oil – 7 tsp
10. Salt and Freshly Ground Pepper – to taste
11. Lamb Loin Chops – 4 1 ¼ inches thick (7 oz. trimmed of excess fat)
12. Water – 1 1/2   cups
13. Cinnamon –1/4 tsp
14. Couscous – 1 cup
15. Chopped Mint – 2 tbsp
16. Chopped Unsalted Pistachios – 2 tbsp

Directions

Preheat the oven to 375 F. Mix 1 tsp olive oil, ½ tsp lemon zest, lemon juice, garlic, cilantro, cayenne, and cumin in a food processor or blender. Season with pepper and salt. Process until you gain a smooth paste. Reserve 1 tbsp.

Spread the paste on lamb chops and let stand for at least 10 minutes before scraping off the seasoning paste.

Bring water to a boil in a small saucepan. Add ½ tsp salt, 1 tbsp olive oil, and cinnamon. Add couscous, lid the skillet and remove from the heat. Let stand for 10 minutes or until all water has been absorbed. Transfer to a large bowl and fluff with a fork. Add pomegranate seeds, remaining lemon zest, pistachios, and mint. Lid and keep warm.

In a medium oven-proof pan, heat 1 tbsp olive oil. Place the lamb chops and cook over moderate heat for 5 minutes or until browned. Turn once. Place the pan in the oven and roast to medium rare (about 6 minutes). Transfer to plate and discard leftover fat.

Add the 1 tbsp of reserved paste and pour pomegranate juice. Set over moderate heat and simmer for 2 minutes or until the liquid reduces to 1/4th cup.

To serve, top the couscous with the lamb chops. Spread sauce on meat, and sprinkle with the remaining pomegranate seeds.

Recipe #10: Roast Lamb Glazed With Pomegranate Sauce

Serving Size

Serves 4

Cooking Time

45 minutes

Nutritional Value

Calories/serving: 317
Total Carbohydrate: 9.6 grams
Cholesterol: 77 mg
Total Fat: 18.8 grams

Ingredients

1. Olive Oil – 2 tsp

2. Boneless Lamb Leg – 1 (1lb trimmed)

3. Kosher Salt – 3/4 tsp (divided)

4. Black Pepper – 1/2 tsp

5. Chopped Onion – 3/4 cup

6. Garlic Cloves – 2 (crushed)

7. Pomegranate Juice – 1/2 cup

8. Balsamic Vinegar – 2 tsp

9. Fat-Free, Reduced-Sodium Chicken Broth – 1 1/2 cups (divided)

10. Sugar – 2 tsp

11. All-Purpose Flour –2 tsp

Directions

Preheat oven to 375 F.

Add oil to a large ovenproof pan and swirl to coat. Heat the oil over medium-high. Season lamb with ½ tsp pepper and salt and add to pan. Sauté for 10 minutes or until each side turns brown. Bake for 15 minutes or until the meat's core 130° is registered on a thermometer. Remove lamb and let stand for 10 minutes to cool.

Replace pan over medium-high heat and sauté for 3 minutes with garlic and onions. Add 1/3 cup pomegranate juice and bring to a boil. Cook further to evaporate all liquid. Pour 1-cup broth, remaining juice, sugar, and ¼ tsp salt. Sir and bring to a boil. Cook for 10 minutes, or till the liquid reduces to ½ cup.

Separately add flour, and the remaining broth. Stir until you gain consistency. Add broth mixture to pan and bring to a boil. Cook while stirring for another minute. Remove from heat and strain. Remove all solids.

Serve lamb with sauce.

Super SHRED Vegetable Recipes

Recipe #1: Cabbage Soup

Serving Size

Serves 4

Cooking Time

20 minutes

Nutritional Value

Calories/serving: 21.9
Total Carbohydrate: 4.9 grams
Cholesterol: 0.0
Total Fat: 0.1 grams

Ingredients

1. Non-Fat Beef Broth – 3 Cups
2. Cabbage – 2 Cups (finely chopped)
3. Yellow Onion –1 small bud
4. Zucchini – ½ Cup (finely chopped)
5. Carrot – ½ Cup (finely chopped)
6. Green Beans – ½ Cup
7. Ground Garlic Clove – 2
8. Tomato Paste – 1 tbsp
9. Oregano – ½ tsp
10. Basil – ½ tsp
11. Salt/Pepper – to taste

Directions

Sauté the carrots, onions, and garlic for 4 to 5 minute in a size-able non-stick pan. Add the broth, beans, and tomato paste to the sauté.

Sprinkle the basil, oregano, salt and paper to your taste. Let the mixture simmer for 8-10 minutes. Add the zucchini when the vegetables are tender and let the mixture simmer for another 5 minutes. Serve.

Recipe #2: Zero Point Italian Soup

Serving Size

Serves 12

Cooking Time

30 minutes

Nutritional Value

Calories/serving: 78.7
Total Carbohydrate: 15.3 grams
Cholesterol: 1.2 mg
Total Fat: 1.2 grams

Ingredients

1. Vegetable Broth – 6 Cups
2. Baby Spinach – 2 Cups
3. Small Zucchini – 2 (sliced and cubed)
4. Escarole – 2 Cups (Chopped)
5. Fennel Bulbs – 2 Cups (thinly slice)
6. Onion – 1 Cup (chopped)
7. Ground Garlic Cloves – 2
8. Red Pepper – 1 (chopped)
9. Red Pepper Flakes – ¼ tsp
10. Diced Tomatoes – 28 oz
11. Oregano – 1 tsp (finely chopped)
12. Fresh Thyme – 2 tsp (finely chopped)
13. Salt – ¾ tsp
14. Black Pepper – ¼ tsp
15. Fresh parsley – ¼ Cup (chopped)
16. Fresh Basil – ¼ Cup

Directions

Add the vegetable broth, garlic, red pepper flakes, thyme, oregano, and red pepper in a large pot. Put the pot on low heat. Add the zucchini, fennel bulb, and diced tomatoes to the pot. Stir and evenly distribute the contents.

Cover the pot and bring to a boil over high heat. After the boil, reduce the heat to low and let the mixture simmer for another 10 minutes. Stir parsley, salt, basil, and black pepper.

Recipe #3: Barley and Vegetable Soup

Serving Size

Serves 6

Good!.

Cooking Time

55 minutes

Nutritional Value

Calories/serving: 75
Total Carbohydrate: 14.3 grams
Cholesterol: 0.0
Total Fat: 0.8 grams

Ingredients

1. Fat-Free Chicken Broth – ~~6~~ 8 Cups
2. Green Cabbage – 2 Cups (chopped)
3. Carrot – 2/3 Cup (finely sliced)
4. Uncooked Barley – 1/3 Cup
5. Onion – ½ Cup (diced)
6. Celery – ½ Cup (sliced)
7. Fresh Parsley – ½ Cup (chopped)
8. Zucchini – 1 (sliced)
9. Garlic Cloves – 2
10. Tomato Paste – ~~1 tbsp~~ ½ can
11. Dried Basil – ½ tsp
12. Dried Thyme – ½ tsp

Directions

Add the sliced celery, carrots, and onion to the non-stick saucepan. Sauté the contents for 7-8 minutes on low heat to get a softened pulp. Sprinkle garlic and stir.

Add the tomato paste and stir the mixture. Add all the herbs, the cabbage, barley, and broth. Simmer the mixture for 20-25 minutes. Add the parsley and zucchini. Cook for another 20 minutes to soften the barley. Adorn with the coarsely ground black pepper.

Recipe #4: Simmered Chicken Lentils

Serving Size

Serves 4

Cooking Time

30 minutes

Nutritional Value

Calories/serving: 103.5
Total Carbohydrate: 14.3 grams
Cholesterol: 0.0
Total Fat: 3 grams

Ingredients

1. Reduced-Sodium Chicken Broth – 1 ½ Cups

2. Lentils – 1 ½ Cups (rinsed, drained, and picked)

3. Carrots – 2 (diced)

4. Olive Oil – 1 tbsp

5. Onion – ½ (medium and chopped)

6. Ground Garlic Cloves – 2

7. Bay Leaves – 2

8. Vinegar – ½ tbsp

9. Salt/Pepper – to taste

Directions

Heat the olive oil in a non-stick pan. Add the garlic, onion, and carrots and sauté for 6-7 minutes until you have a soft pulp. Add the lentils, bay leaves, and the broth to the mixture. Simmer for about 20 minutes to get the lentils tender. Remove the bay leaves.

Season with vinegar, salt and pepper. Serve.

Recipe #5: Brussels Sprouts

Serving Size

Serves 1

Cooking Time

30 minutes

Nutritional Value

Calories/serving: 130.5
Total Carbohydrate: 21.7 grams
Cholesterol: 0.0
Total Fat: 4 grams

Ingredients

1. Fresh Brussels Sprouts –1 ½ lb
2. Onion – 1 large sweet onion
3. Olive Oil – 1 tbsp
4. Fresh Thyme Leaves – 4 tbsp
5. Salt – ¼ tsp
6. Ground Black Pepper – 1/8 tsp

Directions

Quarter the onion into thick slices. Trim the sprouts and remove any yellowed leaves. Slice the sprouts into quarters or halves.

Preheat the oven to 400. Set up a rimmed baking sheet. Add the onions, sprouts, oil, thyme, salt, and pepper to the baking sheet. Roast for about 25 minutes so that the vegetables are tender. Occasionally stir to prevent any charring. Serve when the vegetables are tender and browned.

Recipe #6: Curried Yellow Split-Pea Soup

Serving Size

Serves 4

Cooking Time

2 hrs 20 minutes

Nutritional Value

Calories/serving: 127.5
Total Carbohydrate: 20.5 grams
Cholesterol: 0.0
Total Fat: 2.4 grams

Ingredients

1. Water – 8 Cups
2. Large Carrot – 1 (finely chopped)
3. Dried Yellow Spilt Peas – 1 Cup
4. Celery – ½ (chopped)
5. Green Peas – ½ Cup (fresh/frozen)
6. Red Bell Pepper – ½ Cup (diced)
7. Low- Fat Yogurt – ½ Cup (plain)
8. Dill Sprigs – ¼ Cup (chopped)
9. Ground Black Pepper – a pinch
10. Salt/pepper – to taste
11. Curry Powder – 1 tbsp
12. Ground Garlic Clove – 1
13. Olive Oil – 2 tbsp

Directions

Add the celery, carrot, onion, garlic, olive oil, and 1 tbsp of water in a 4 quart saucepan. Mix and cook the contents over low heat for 10 minutes or till they have softened. Stir often to avoid browning or charring.

Add the curry powder. Mix and cook for another minute. Pour 8 cups of water and add the split peas. Bring the mixture to a boil. Leave the contents to simmer and cook on medium-low heat for 2 hours or until the soup has thickened and the peas are tender.

Add the peppers and salt to taste. Mix in peas and bell pepper and cook for another 5 minutes or till all the vegetables are tender. Pour the soup in shallow bowls. Mix the Low- Fat Yogurt and dill in a separate bowl. Add it to each bowl of soup to taste.

Recipe #7: Pumpkin Ravioli

Serving Size

Serves 6

Cooking Time

15 minutes

Nutritional Value

Calories/serving: 162
Total Carbohydrate: 22 grams
Cholesterol: 17 mg
Total Fat: 5 grams

Ingredients

1. Canned Pumpkin – 1 cup

2. Parmesan cheese – 1/3 cup (grated)

3. Chicken Broth – 1/2 cup

4. Unsalted Butter – 1 1/2 tablespoons

5. Wonton Wrappers – 24

6. Salt – 1/4 tsp

7. Black Pepper – 1/8 tsp

8. Salt – 1 tsp

9. Parsley – Chopped

Directions

Mix 1/3 cup parmesan with 1-cup pumpkin, salt, and black pepper. Use water to moisten the edges of the dough. Spoon spread 2 tbsp of pumpkin mixture on the center of each wonton wrapper. Fold the sides and join the edges to form a triangle.

In a large saucepan of boiling water, place the ravioli. Sprinkle 1 tsp salt. Cook for 7 minutes, and drain. Mix the butter and 1/2 cup broth in a pan and bring to a boil. Toss ravioli. Sprinkle parsley. Serve.

Recipe #8: A Warm Dip of Artichoke and Spinach

Serving Size

Serves 32

Cooking Time

25 minutes

Nutritional Value

Calories/serving: 59
Total Carbohydrate: 4 grams
Cholesterol: 5 mg
Total Fat: 4 grams

Ingredients

1. Artichoke Hearts – 1 Can (14 oz. drained)
2. Lima/Butter beans – 1 Can (16 oz. drained)
3. Fat-Free Cream Cheese – 4 oz. (tub style)
4. Light Mayonnaise – 1 cup
5. Pre-shredded part-skim mozzarella cheese –3/4 cup
6. Grated Parmesan Cheese – 1/4 cup
7. Frozen Chopped Spinach – 1 pack (10 oz. thawed, drained, and squeezed dry)
8. Hot Pepper Sauce – 1 tsp
9. Extra-Virgin Olive Oil – 1 tbsp
10. Capers – 1 tsp (drained)
11. Freshly Ground Black Pepper – 1/4 tsp
12. Dry Mustard – 1/4 tsp
13. Sliced Green Onions – 1/2 cup
14. Fresh Lemon Juice – 1 tsp

Directions

Preheat oven to 350F.

Mix the artichoke hearts, spinach, mozzarella and parmesan cheese, green onions, and lemon juice in a bowl. Add the remaining ingredients to a food processor. Process till you have a smooth puree. Add the artichoke-cheese mixture to the processor. Process the contents until you have a consistent puree. Spread the mixture evenly onto a 1-quart casserole dish.

Bake in oven for 30 minutes or until the edges bloom. Remove from oven. Allow to cool for a few minutes. Serve.

Recipe #9: Brussels Sprouts Roasted with Pecans

Serving Size

Serves 5

Cooking Time

45 minutes

Nutritional Value

Calories/serving: 168
Total Carbohydrate: 11 grams
Cholesterol: 0.0
Total Fat: 13 grams

Ingredients

1. Brussels sprouts – 2 lbs (trimmed and halved)
2. Pecans – 1 cup (roughly chopped)
3. Olive Oil – 2 tbsp
4. Cloves Garlic – 2 (finely chopped)
5. Kosher Salt and Black Pepper – to taste

Directions

Heat the oven to 400 F. On a large rimmed baking sheet, toss the pecans, oil, garlic, with Brussels sprouts. Sprinkle ¼ tsp pepper, and ½ tsp salt. Toss again. Arrange the sprouts with their cut-side towards the baking sheet. Roast for 20 – 25 minutes or until they become golden brown and tender. Remove from oven and Serve!

Recipe #10: Caramelized-Shallot Strudel with Mushrooms

Serving Size

Serves 8

Cooking Time

50 minutes

Nutritional Value

Calories/serving: 176
Total Carbohydrate: 24.9 grams
Cholesterol: 11 mg
Total Fat: 5.5 grams

Ingredients

1. Olive Oil – 1 tsp

2. Sliced Shallots – 1 ½ cups (8 oz.)

3. Dry Breadcrumbs – 1/3 cup

4. Sugar – 1/8 tsp

5. Water – 1 tbsp

6. Pre-sliced Mushrooms – 4 packs (8 oz. each)

7. Dry Marsala/Madeira – 2 tbsp

8. Low-Fat Sour Cream – 2/3 cup

9. Chopped Fresh Parsley – 1/4 cup

10. Salt – 1/2 tsp

11. Dried Thyme – 1/4 teaspoon

12. Freshly Ground Black Pepper – 1/4 tsp

13. Frozen Phyllo Dough – 8 sheets (thawed)

14. Butter – 1 tbsp (melted)

Directions

In a large non-stick pan, heat the oil on medium-high heat. Sprinkle sugar and add shallots. Cook while stirring for 2 minutes. Sprinkle water and lid the pan. Cook with occasional stirs for 10 minutes on medium-low heat or until the shallots become tender.

With the pan uncovered, add and cook mushrooms over medium-high for 20 minutes or until most of the liquid evaporates. Next add and cook with Marsala for a minute. Remove from heat, and let the mushroom mixture cool. Stir in thyme, parsley, sour cream, salt, and pepper. Reserve ¼ cups of the mixture.

Preheat the oven to 400 F.

On a large cutting board, lightly coat a phyllo sheet with cooking spray. Sprinkle 2 tsp breadcrumbs and repeat layers for 3 additional phyllo sheets. Along the long edge of the phyllo, spoon spread the mushroom mixture leaving 1-inch along the borders. Roll the phyllo in jellyroll style. Start at the long edge.

Coat a baking sheet with cooking spray. With its seam-side downwards, place the strudel on a baking sheet. Repeat similar procedure with remaining phyllo sheets. End by tucking their ends under them. Butter the strudels and bake for 20 minutes.

Remove from oven and let stand for 5 minutes. Slice the strudel in 3-5 slices before serving.

Conclusion

With this we have come to the end of this report. Over the course of this report you came across five different categories of recipes for your super SHRED diet plan. Each category was based on its main ingredient. These included chicken, beef, seafood, lamb, and vegetables.

Each category comprised of 10 different recipes. Each recipe was selected or designed to meet all the requirements of the super SHRED diet plan of Dr. Ian Smith. We hope to have conveyed the ingredients and the cooking directions as simply and fluently as possible.

With this, we wish you all the best for your Super Shredding endeavors. All the best!

Made in the USA
San Bernardino, CA
04 September 2014